Christmas Haiku Poetry
By Colleen White

CW Butterfly Publishing
Dallas, Texas

DEDICATION

This collection of Haiku poetry is dedicated to my family. However, the greatest Haiku poet is Japanese Haiku master, Matsuo Basho. My favorite Haiku poem by him is entitled, "The Old Pond".

Winter

Laughter fills the air.
Happy children sing, laugh, shout!
Snowflakes dance around.

Snow

Melting gently—snow.
Softly falling down on hair.
The winter has come.

Christmas Tree

Twinkle lights shine bright.
Ornaments placed sweetly there.
Gifts under the tree.

Nutcracker

The nutcracker dances.
Ballerinas twirl and twirl.
It leaps high and wide.

Ornament

A glass ornament.
He gave it to me that day.
It was an angel.

Prickly Tree

A prickly green tree.
Filled the space with a sweet scent.
The small children laughed.

Angels

Angels fly high above.
They hear prayers from below.
Whispers sent with love.

Candy Canes

Red and white candy.
She licks each one hurriedly.
Christmas day laughter.

Sunday Morning

Christmas morning comes.
Sunday morning church worship.
Pastor sings and shouts!

Christmas Candle

The light shines brightly.
It sways in the wind softly.
Today is Christmas.

Deer

The deer in the woods.
Stood tall and proud in the snow.
It stared at me long.

Christmas Gifts

Wrapped Christmas gifts glisten.
They rest gently under trees.
Bright bows bounce on top.

Crunch

Crunch, crunch, crunch hard snow.
Slide, glide, twirl on icy snow.
Moving fast across.

Snowglobe

Snow fills the circle.
Perfectly round and snowy.
The snowglobe is bright.

Snowman

Snowman, snowman smile.
Watch little children play now.
Handsome snowman falls.

Church

Precious little white church.
Plain cross atop of the steeple.
People kneel to pray.

Faith

Stillness fills the air.
People long for joy and peace.
Faith in One more wise.

Church Bells

Church bells ring loudly.
Members sit on pews and pray.
Christmas bells ring strong.

Sleigh Bells

Sleigh bells clang loudly.
People stare enviously.
Snow falls upon heads.

ABOUT THE AUTHOR

Colleen White, is an author, poet, painter, and educator. She enjoys writing, painting, reading, and spending time with her family. She has written over twenty books, a mixture of novels, novellas, children stories, and poetry.

A few of her popular books are the following:
- *A Special Christmas (a romance novel)*
- *My Psalms: A Collection of Poetry (poetry about faith)*
- *Kevin the Christmas Cat (a children's story)*
- *Ezra and Kate: A Love Story (A Story of Faith)*

- *All books are available on Amazon.*
- *Subscribe to Dr. White's YouTube Channel, Dr. White's Reading Corner.*

"Christmas Poetry is for the Heart and Soul." –Dr. Colleen White

Enjoy the Holidays! Merry Christmas.

Snowflakes…Soft and Wet…Snowflakes dance their dance.

Snowman smiled at me. He Sang a song for me and kept my dreams free.

Winter storm–trees look like ghosts. Ice hangs low and nowhere to go.

Little red glass globe placed on the tree. Little red glass globe dances on the tree.

Jolly Saint Nick laughs aloud. His red nose looks like a bow set on a cloud. Laughing at Santa is enough for me.

Bells will sing and ring the lovely sound of Christmas.

Tender snow covers the branches. The pearly white snow covers red glass spheres too. They move through the wind gently looking like jewels in the sky.

This Little Tree

As the air is getting colder and the holidays draw near,
We all find ways to show we care and spread our Christmas cheer.
The grown-ups hustle-bustle and the city glows with light,
But the children look for smaller ways to make the season bright:

We share our smiles and laughter with the people that we see.
We sing our favorite Christmas songs and decorate the tree.
We think about the blessings we enjoy the whole year through,
And hope for peace and happiness to shine on friends like you.

As we hang each shining ornament right up to Christmas Day,
This little tree reminds us of the role we children play:
For though it's small, each bauble brings a special kind of joy
Just like the Christmas spirit in each little girl and boy.

O Christmas Tree

German Folk Song

I Heard the Bells on Christmas Day

HENRY W. LONGFELLOW, 1863

J. BAPTISTE CALKIN, 1872

1. I heard the bells on Christ-mas day Their
2. I thought how, as the day had come, The
3. And in des-pair I bow'd my head, "There
4. Then pealed the bells more loud and deep, "God

old fa-mil-iar car-ols play, And wild and sweet the
bel-fries of all Christ-en-dom Had roll'd a-long the
is no peace on earth," I said, For hate is strong and
is not dead, nor doth he sleep, The wrong shall fail, the

words re-peat Of peace on earth good will to men.
bro-ken song Of peace on earth good will to men.
mocks the song Of peace on earth good will to men.
right pre-vail, With peace on earth good will to men."

CHRISTMAS SONG.

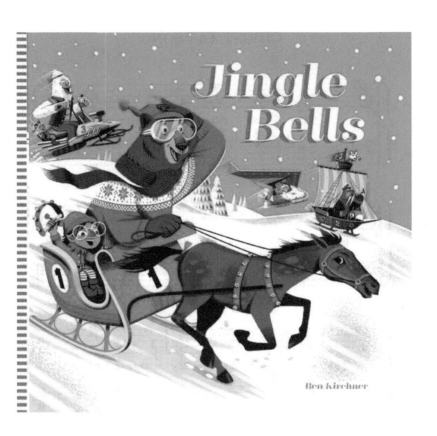

Jingle Bells

Ben Kirchner

Christmas
Greetings

ye
Olde tyme
Christmas
Dinner

Tis The Season to be Joyful…..

Write Your Own Joyful Haiku Below.

1.
2.
3.

Christmas is a Season of Giving…

Reflect about what Christmas means to you.

Write a paragraph below.

Journal About Christmas…

Journal About Peace in the World below…

Journal About How You Can Help Someone This Christmas.

This is the Season of Advent… Journal about what this means to you.

How are You Preparing for Christmas? Journal below.

Love is the True Spirit of Christmas… Journal about it.

Do you Believe in the Magic of Christmas? Journal about it.

How are You Going to be Jolly this Season? Journal about it.

How Can You Be Joyful This Christmas? Journal about it below.

What are you thankful for? Journal below.

Who are You Thankful For? Journal Below.

What Did You Have to Overcome this Year? Journal below.

Take a minute to reflect about where you are in your life and journal about it below.

Write Your Christmas Wish List below.

1.
2.
3.
4.
5.
6.

Write Your Christmas Wish List for Our Country below.

1.
2.
3.
4.
5.
6.

Write Your Christmas Wish List for the World below.

1.

2.

3.

4.

5.

6.

Write Your Holiday To Do List Below.

1.
2.
3.
4.
5.
6.

MERRY CHRISTMAS AND HAPPY NEW YEAR!

Made in United States
North Haven, CT
15 December 2024

62653733R00046